Portland, Oregon is a city that embraces its differences and sits juxtaposed to its rich natural surroundings. It's a hub for the ingenious, a haven for the many creative minds that populate its galleries, restaurants, studios, and storefronts, each as intriguing as the last. It's home to some of the leading names in the creative and tech industries, as well as a number of the most sought-after thinkers in the country, which has helped to set the scene for a city of brilliant design as well as a world-class dining scene. If you're looking for a multifaceted city for a creative adventure, you've found it!

CITIx60: Portland explores one of US' greenest and hippest cities through the eyes of 60 creative stars. Together, they take you on a journey through the best in architecture, art spaces, shopping, cuisine and entertainment. This guide will lead you on an authentic tour of Portland that gets to the heart of what locals love most about their city.

Contents

D1173064

Before You Go

BASIC INFO

Currency
U.S. Dollar (USD/$)
Exchange rate: US$1 : €0.8

Time zone
GMT -8
DST -7

DST begins at 0200 (local time) on the second Sunday of March and ends at 0300 (local time) on the first Sunday of November.

Dialling
International calling: +1
Citywide: 503, 971

*Always include area code for calls. Dial 1 for domestic calls, or 001 for calls made outside the US.

Weather (avg. temperature range)
Spring (Mar-May): 4-21°C / 39-69°F
Summer (Jun-Aug): 21-30°C / 69-86°F
Autumn (Sep-Nov): 5-14°C / 41-58°F
Winter (Dec-Feb): -1-12°C / 30-54°F

USEFUL WEBSITES

Public transport news and journey planner
trimet.org

Real-time traffic and road conditions
www.tripcheck.com

EMERGENCY CALLS

Ambulance, fire or police
911

Non-emergency police
+1 (503) 823 3333

Consulates
Japan   +1 (503) 221 1811
Thailand   +1 (503) 221 0440
Denmark   +1 (503) 802 2131
France   +1 (503) 746 6779
Germany   +1 (503) 222 0490

AIRPORT EXPRESS TRANSFER

Portland International Airport (PDX) <-> Pioneer Square (MAX Light Rail Red Line)
Trains / Journey: every 15 mins / 38 mins
From PDX – 0442-2308
From Pioneer Square – 0357-2230
One-way: $2.50/$1.25
trimet.org

PUBLIC TRANSPORT IN PORTLAND

Max Light Rail
WES Commuter Rail
Portland Streetcar
Portland Aerial Tram
Bus
Bike
Taxi

Means of Payment
Cash
Credit cards

Single-journey tickets allow unlimited rides within 2.5 hours on Max Light Rail, WES Commuter Rail, Portland Streetcar and buses.

PUBLIC HOLIDAYS

January	1 New Year's Day, Martin Luther King Jr. Day (3rd Mon)
February	Presidents' Day (3rd Mon)
May	Memorial Day (Last Mon)
July	4 Independence Day
September	Labour Day (1st Mon)
November	11 Veterans Day, Thanksgiving Day (4th Thu)
December	25 Christmas Day

If a holiday falls on a weekend, the closest weekday becomes a 'substitute' day. Museums, galleries and shops are likely to be closed or operate on special hours on Thanksgiving, Christmas Eve, Christmas Day, New Year's Day, and Independence Day.

FESTIVALS / EVENTS

January
Portland Fine Print Fair
www.portlandfineprintfair.com

February
Portland International Film Festival
nwfilm.org/festivals/piff
PDX Jazz
www.pdxjazz.com

April
Design Week Portland
designweekportland.com

May
Filmed By Bike
filmedbybike.org
Cinco de Mayo Fiesta
www.cincodemayo.org

June
Pride North West
pridenw.org
Quiet Music Festival
www.quietmusicfestivalofportland.com

July
Mississippi Street Fair
mississippiave.com
Northwest String Summit
stringsummit.com
What The Festival
whatthefestival.com

August
Forest For The Trees (#19)
www.forestforthetreesnw.com
Pickathon
www.pickathon.com
Project Pabst
portland.projectpabst.com
Stay Wild Festival
www.staywildmagazine.com/expo

Event days vary by year. Please check for
updates online.

UNUSUAL OUTINGS

BrewCycle
www.brewgrouppdx.com

Beer Quest Walking Tours
beerquestpdx.com

Shanghai Tunnels
www.shanghaitunnels.info

Beyond Bizarre Tour
FB: Beyond Bizarre Tour

Pedal Bike Tours
pedalbiketours.com

SMARTPHONE APP

Official public transport ticketing service
TriMet Tickets

Real-time traffic & travel planner
PDX Transit, Transit App

Food cart tracker
CartCompass (iOS only)

REGULAR EXPENSES

Newspaper
$2-5

Domestic / international mail (postcards)
$0.49/$1.15

Gratuities
Diners: 15-20% for waitstaff & bartenders
Hotels: $1-2@bag for porter, $1-5 daily for
cleaners
Licensed taxis: 15-20%

Count to 10

What makes Portland so special?

Illustrations by Guillaume Kashima aka Funny Fun

Portland is an organically-curated destination, filled with innovative people blazing a trail to an urban experience that is more than what the average city has to offer while surrounded by some of the most beautiful natural landscapes in the country. Whether you're here for a day or a week, see what Portland's creative class considers an essential to-do list.

1

Hike Routes

Angel's Rest
A 2.4 mile-hike up for the scenic views of the Columbia River Gorge

Trail of Ten Falls
A moderate 7.2 mile loop hike

Forest Park (#3)
One of the country's largest urban forest reserves

Wahclella Falls Hike
A 2-mile family-friendly round trip

Latourell Falls Hike
A 2.4-mile hike, featured in John Hillcoat's movie The Road (2009)

Multnomah Falls Hike
A 2.6-mile loop trip for spectacular views of the falls & gorge scenery

Rocky Butte Hike
A 3.2-mile in-and-out hike for sunset & a 360° view of the city from the extinct volcanic cinder cone butte

2
Closer to Nature

Ride a bike
On the city's abundant bike lanes, over the bridges and along the Willamette

Vaux's Swift watch in fall
audubonportland.org/
local-birding/swiftwatch

Small farms, wildlife & beaches
Sauvie Island, sauvieisland.org

Wineries & pick-your-own farm
hoodriverfruitloop.com

Hunt for edible mushrooms
With *All That The Rain Promises & More* (1991) by David Arora

Mt St Helens Ape Caves
www.fs.usda.gov/recarea/
giffordpinchot.recarea/?recid=40393

Ecola State Park (Oregon Coast), Timberline Lodge (Mt. Hood)
Beautiful scenery within 90 minutes' drive from Portland

3
Parks

Bridges & sunset
The Skidmore Bluffs
2230 N Skidmore Ct., OR 97217

Fresh air, peace, birds & squirrels
Crystal Springs
Rhododendron Garden
5801 SE 28th Ave., OR 97202

World's tiniest park
Mill Ends Park
SW Taylor St., OR 97204

**Nude beach &
views of the Columbia River Gorge**
Rooster Rock State Park
Exit 25 & Hwy. 84, Corbett, OR 97019

Zoo, forestry museum, arboretum, children's museum & rose garden
4001 SW Canyon Rd., OR 97221

4
Street Mural Hunt

Keep Portland Weird
350 W Burnside St., OR 97209
www.keepportlandweird.com

**Hey, Girl
by Alexander Barret &
Blakely Dadson**
NE Glisan St. & NE 24th Ave., OR 97232

**Everything is Everything
by Zach Yarrington**
2121 SE 6th Ave., OR 97214

Other Hand by Olivia Knapp
7804 SE Stark St., OR 97215

**Forest For The Trees
by Michael Reeder**
1129 SW Washington St., OR 97205

**Star Catcher
by Rustam QBic**
1005 SW Park Ave., OR 97205

5

Breakfast & Brunch Spots

Tasty N Alder, Tasty N Sons
0900–1430 daily, sit-in only
www.tastynalder.com

Broder Nord
0800–1500 daily
www.broderpdx.com

Sweedeedee (#46)

Roost
1000–1400 Sa & Su
www.roostpdx.com

Old Salt
0900–1500 Sa & Su
www.oldsaltpdx.com

King Farmers Market
Sundays only
www.portlandfarmersmarket.org

Simpatica Dining Hall
0900–1400 Sundays
www.simpaticapdx.com

6

Portland Staples

Homemade buttery, flaky biscuits
Pine State Biscuits
www.pinestatebiscuits.com

Wings
Pok Pok Noi, www.pokpoknoi.com

Pastry
Roman Candle
www.romancandlebaking.com

Fried Chicken
Screen Door
www.screendoorrestaurant.com

**Seasonal & unique
ice cream flavors**
Salt & Straw, saltandstraw.com

Chicken & Rice
Nong's Khao Man Gai (#44)

**Fried Chicken Phở Đặc Biệt (Pho
Special) & Phở Chay Đậu Hủ (Pho
Vegetarian)**
Phở Lê (#43)

7

Tea & Coffee Points

Courier Coffee Roasters
www.couriercofeeroasters.com

Heart Coffee for Chai
heartroasters.com

**Extracto Coffee Roasters for
very strong coffee & bagels**
www.extractcoffee.com

Good Coffee for Cortado
goodcoffeepdx.com

**Coquine for a romantic
neighborhood vibe**
coquinepdx.com

**Café Castagna for smart, season
driven menus & patio**
www.castagnarestaurant.com

**Café Castagna for Coffee with
house-made alternative milk**
upperleftroasters.com

**See See Motor Coffee for custom
bikes & Stumptown coffee**
www.seeseemotorcycles.com

8

Locally Made

From jewelry & home goods
to motorcycles & kayaks
MadeHere PDX, madeherepdx.com

Soaps hand-crafted with
natural & local ingredients
Maak Lab, www.maaklab.com

Handmade accessories
crafted with Japanese textiles
Kiriko, www.kirikomade.com

Products, tools & resources
around woodwork
Woodcrafters, woodcrafters.us

Portland & rare designer labels
Frances May, francesmay.com

Trending news & events
about local breweries, cideries &
distilleries
Brewpublic, www.brewpublic.com

9

Books

Artworks, found
photography, printed ephemera
& works on paper
Ampersand
www.ampersandgallerypdx.com

Clean & organised
graphic novels & comics
Bridge City Comics
www.bridgecitycomics.com

Nicely curated art books
Monograph Bookwerks
www.monographbookwerks.com

Books printed & bound
on demand
Publication Studio (#25)

Centuries-old novels &
first editions
Powell's antique books section
www.powells.com

10

Everything Vintage

19th & 20th-century
vehicular & die-cast toys
Kidd's Toy Museum
www.kiddstoymuseum.com

Pendletons, dresses & boots
Animal Traffic
www.animaltrafficpdx.com

Vintage records
Crossroads Music, www.xro.com

Musical instruments
Old Town Music
www.oldtownmusicportland.com

Hard-to-find cameras &
equipment
Hollywood Camera Store
4039 NE Sandy Blvd., OR 97212

Records, magazines, photos,
maps & movie posters
SMUT
www.smutportland.blogspot.com

Icon Index

 Opening hours

 Admission

 Address

 Facebook

 Contact

 Website

 Remarks

 Scan QR codes to access Google Maps and discover the area around each destination. Internet connection required.

60x60

60 Local Creatives x 60 Hotspots

From vast cityscapes to the tiniest glimpses of everyday exchanges, there's always something to provoke your imagination. 60X60 points you to 60 haunts where 60 arbiters of taste cut their teeth.

Landmarks & Architecture

SPOTS · 01 – 12

Refresh yourself in a city saturated with scenic landscapes, convenient hiking, and bike trails that run through industrial parks and comb the edges of beautiful Pacific Northwest Rivers.

Cultural & Art Spaces

SPOTS · 13 – 24

Portland's creative energy takes influence from every corner of the globe, and is visible in all of its industries. It's a haven for artistic expression, which can be found blossoming across the city.

Markets & Shops

SPOTS · 25 – 36

Shopping locally is an embodiment of Portland's ideals which has inspired heaps of niche design studios, music stores, craft and clothing shops, and even specialty grocers.

Restaurants & Cafés

SPOTS · 37 – 48

It's hard to go wrong with the food, drinks, and especially coffee in Portland. With the many intricate options, an undeniably delicious adventure awaits at every kitchen, bar and café.

Nightlife

SPOTS · 49 – 60

From a calm night spent under the stars or at a rooftop bar to an energetic laser-lit dance floor and everything in between, nightlife in "PDX" can satisfy anyone's cravings.

Landmarks & Architecture

Beautiful horizons, epic views and efficiently designed structures

Portland is a green city in every sense of the word, overflowing with beautiful parks, structures designed for aesthetic and practical efficiency, and bicycle-friendly streets, with everything placing the environment first. Named by Francis Pettygrove after his home-town of Portland, Maine in 1845, the original settlement grew out of its easy access to water-based shipping routes in the 1830s, making Portland a port town and a hub for large shipments of timber. The Willamette River flows north through the city, splitting it into the "east" and "west" sections that have become signifiers for getting around many of the neighborhoods. The river's position through downtown has created a cityscape defined by bridges, many of which are over 100 years old (and all of which are still heavily used by locals and commuters). One of these is the gorgeous Fremont Bridge, which sits high in the sky above the Willamette River at the northern end of the city and is the second longest tie-arch bridge in the world. Much of downtown Portland is also relatively flat, thanks to its position between foothills and three surrounding mountain ranges. Over the year these western foothills have transformed into an alluring neighborhood woven into the sloping landscape, featuring popular destinations like Forest Park and several beautifully designed homes overlooking the city.

Modi Oyewole
Co-founder, Trillectro

The self-professed "Pharrell Stan" wears his passions, interests and opinions on his sleeve. It's this worldview that helped Modi bring unforgettable experiences to his city.

4T Trail
P.015

Jim Golden
Photographer

Specializing in still life and product photography, Golden brings an artist's eye and an enthusiast's passion to his work, and strives to capture the pared-down essence of his subjects.

Public-Library
Design studio

With offices in LA and Portland, Public-Library was founded in 2011 as a space to construct identities and compose digital experiences, translating thought into meaningful solutions.

Tom McCall Waterfront Park P.014

Forest Park P.016

Oblio
Digital agency

Oblio specializes in the use of technologies as a design tool. Our team of inventors, artists, designers, and developers has worked on over 50 major motion picture campaigns.

Portland Japanese Garden P.020

Spencer Staley
Founder, The Good Mod

I am a designer and artist. My motto is "always be researching".

Nicholas Ross
Creative director, GUILD

Ross makes his way to Portland by way of alternative design education and practice and collaborates with groundbreaking designers on subversions, machinations, and events.

Columbia River Scenic Highway P.017

Portland Oregon Temple P.022

Jennifer James Wright
Art director & designer

I'm originally from the Lone Star State. I've most recently worked at Wieden+Kennedy and is now the Design Director at Ouur, the publisher behind Kinfolk Magazine.

Cathedral Park
P.024

Pantelis Kosmas
Mars Water

Portland native Pantelis Kosmas is a school counselor by day, and frontman of the local band Mars Water by night. He and his wife own high quality, handmade skin product brand Kosmas Co.

Damien Gilley
Artist & professor

I work in large-scale installation and drawing, often combining themes of deconstructed architectures and manipulated perspectives. I also teach at the Pacific Northwest College of Art.

The Grotto
P.023

Ira Keller Fountain
P.025

Keri Elmsly
Creative director, Second Story

I drive the evolution and execution of Second Story's creative vision. My experience traverses public art, large-scale interactive installations, touring shows, and gallery works.

Oaks Park
P.028

Kayla Mattes
Textile artist

I live and work in Portland, Oregon. My woven tapestries and installations are primarily influenced by a blend of pop-culture, the internet, color, and consumerism.

Arthur Hitchcock
Photographer & art director

My specialties are documentary photography and environmental portraiture. Originally from the Midwest, raised in Long Beach and now rooted in Portland. I am a nomad and a day-dreamer.

Willamette Falls & Municipal Elevator
P.026

Mount Angel Abbey Library
P.029

1 Tom McCall Waterfront Park
Map C, P.103

Home to eye-catching cherry blossoms in spring, countless festivals and concerts during summer, and a perfect spot for jogs mixed with people watching in fall or winter, the stretch of greenery is a perfect year-round Portland destination. If you're here between March and December, check out the Saturday Market at 2 SW Naito Parkway for everything from fresh-picked Lavender shrubs to Elephant Ears. In June, snap your best Instagram of the ferris wheel from Portland Rose Festival from the northeast side of the Hawthorne Bridge. The northeast side of the Burnside Bridge offers the best view of the freshly bloomed greenery in spring and famous white stag sign.

🕓 *0500–0000 daily*
🏠 *Naito Pkwy., OR 97201*
🔗 *www.portlandoregon.gov*

"It's solid for people-watching and worth taking a stroll around the Waterfront. Check the views from the surrounding bridges, too!"

– Modi Oyewole, Trillectro

2 4T Trail
Map C, P.102

Hands down the best way to explore the west side of Portland, especially if you don't drive, is to experience the 4T loop made up of a trail and rides on a tram, a trolley, and a train. Through public transport and good old-fashioned walking, you'll get to see a varying landscape that takes you from the heart of downtown, to Council Crest, the highest point in the city, with a few elephants and bears along the way at the Oregon Zoo. Be prepared to dedicate the majority of your day for this adventure as the trail portion alone is close to four miles.

🕐 ⓢ *Tram ($4.50): 0530-2130 (M-F), 0900-1700 (Sa), 1300-1700 (Su, May 22-Sep 18), Trolley (streetcar, $2): 0545-2330 (M-F), 0730- (Sa), 0730-2230 (Su), Train (MAX Light Rail, $2.50/1.25): schedule varies with days*
🔗 *4ttrail.wordpress.com*

"Exercise, ride the tram, and see the views of downtown and the Cascade mountains from Council Crest. Wear good shoes for hikes and dress in layers."

– Jim Golden

3 Forest Park
Map S, P.109

As part of the Tualatin Mountains, Forest Park is one of Oregon's many natural and breathtaking forests. What makes this one special is its convenience to inner city Portlanders and visitors, with more than 80 miles of walkable, bikeable and dog friendly trails to break away from the daily grind. One way to get to the historic Pittock Mansion for sweeping downtown views from the highest point in the park is to take Wildwood Trail that starts from Washington Park at its south end. Consider also a visit to Hoyt Arboretum for a stroll among the rare trees. Early morning or at sunset is a nice time to go.

🕐 0500-2200 daily
URL www.forestparkconservancy.org
🔗 Wildwood spur trail along Japanese Garden's service road remains closed until April 1 2017

"Get lost! There is so much to see and explore here. "
– Public-Library

4 Columbia River Scenic Highway

Map AA, P.110

Less than 30 minutes from the city, the Columbia River Scenic highway is the nation's oldest scenic highway and one of the Seven Wonders of Oregon. A 75-mile journey stretches between downtown Troutdale and The Dalles, which runs through the Columbia River Gorge. Take Interstate 84 East for about 20 miles and get off on the Columbia River Scenic highway and be greeted by a multitude of hiking trailheads and waterfalls, including the infamous Multnomah Falls, the second tallest year round waterfall in the United States.

🏠 *Troutdale, OR 97060 – The Dalles, OR 97058*
🔗 *columbiariverhighway.com*

"This is why we love Portland. Because places like this help us get away and get inspired."

– Oblio

5 Portland Japanese Garden
Map B, P.102

An amalgamation of five themed gardens, sprawling across a total of 9.1 acres, the Portland Japanese Garden was crafted in the early 1960s to pay homage to "Japanese culture, tradition, and aesthetics" and provide awareness toward environmental sustainability. Each of the five gardens has their own unique characteristics that help drive the notions of peace and tranquility from waterfalls to traditional tea ceremonies in an authentic tea room. Right across the road is the International Rose Test Garden where more than 500 rose varieties are planted and tested. Roses normally blooms from April to October and peaks in June, and locals celebrate with parades and fireworks.

🕐 Mar 13–Sep 30: 1200–1900 (M), 1000– (Tu–Su), Oct 1–Feb 13: 1200–1600 (M), 1000– (Tu–Su)
💲 $9.50/7.75/6.75
🏠 611 SW Kingston Ave., OR 97205
🔗 japanesegarden.com

"This is a very relaxing to go. Go on a weekday for less crowds. It changes dramatically through the seasons and is worth multiple visits."
– Spencer Staley, The Good Mod

6 Portland Oregon Temple
Map X, P.110

With a white marble construction, lush gardens, and an infinity pool surrounded by Douglas-fir trees, the Portland Oregon Temple might literally be a slice of heaven. With an impossibly white exterior and six spires reaching into the sky the grounds are a breathtaking sight. Belonging to the Church of Jesus Christ of Latter-day Saints, the temple is the first of its kind to be constructed in the state of Oregon. Only since 2012 has the space added

public operating hours for those who fancy impressive post-war architecture or a thoroughly peaceful experience.

Visitors' Center: 0900-2100 daily
13600 SW Kruse Oaks Blvd., Lake Oswego, OR 97035-8602
+1 (503) 639 7066
URL www.ldschurchtemples.com

"You don't have to be religious to appreciate the pristine white fantasy looking spires rising out of the equally storybook grounds."

– Nicholas Ross, Guild

7 The Grotto
Map U, P.109

A functioning Roman Catholic shrine otherwise known as Sanctuary of our Sorrowful Mother, The Grotto stands in incredibly beautiful grounds in Northeast Portland surrounded by tall Oregon trees and moss. With its main chapel placed in a carved-out cave at the side of a cliff face, the unique site offers an ultimate calming space, attracting young couples to come tie the knot. The upper levels of the sanctuary holds a botanical garden that also provides view points to many of the surrounding mountains and valleys.

🕐 0900-2030 daily
💲 Upper level garden: $6/5/3
🏠 8840 NE Skidmore St., OR 97220
📞 +1 (503) 254 7371 🔗 thegrotto.org
🎫 Free guided tour (Sa-Su): 1130, 1400

"There's an elevator that will take you to the upper gardens. To ride it, stop into the gift shop at the ground's entrance and buy a ticket at the cashier."
– Jennifer James Wright

8 Cathedral Park
Map Q, P.109

With the tree-lined horizon, sun reflecting off of the Willamette River, and St. Johns Bridge looming overhead, this is the perfect park for a weekend picnic or casual stroll. The stairs underneath the east side of the bridge, facing west, is a favorite vantage point. If you have dogs, this is a perfect summertime watering hole for them to cool off at as a section of the river, by the floating pier, has a barricade that keeps your pets safe from the current. Look for Tienda Santa Cruz nearby at 8630 N Lombard St. Inside the Mexican grocery store hides a popular spot for authentic tacos.

🕐 *0500–0000 daily*
🏠 *N Edison St. & Pittsburg Ave., OR 97203*

"This is my favorite bridge in Portland. My wife and I got engaged under this bridge. Bring a camera!"

– Pantelis Kosmas, Mars Water

9 Ira Keller Fountain

Map E, P.104

Proposed by Lawrence Halprin, who also designed San Francisco's Ghirardelli Square, Ira Keller Fountain was built in 1970 to battle urban blight in downtown Portland. Over ten thousand gallons of water are dispersed by the minute to ensure optimal water splashing by children and feet dipping into the pools by adults. Together with three other interactive fountains, starting from the southernmost Source Fountain, the spaces collectively celebrate nature and form the notable Open Space Sequence. Welcome to the perfect place to cool off and relax to the sound of a waterfall right in the middle of the city.

🏠 SW 3rd Ave. & Clay St., OR 97201
🔗 www.portlandoregon.gov

"Go on a cloudy summer morning! Sunny days and weekends especially are too crowded, and it is 'off' in winter."

– Damien Gilley

10 Willamette Falls & Municipal Elevator

Map W, P.110

If you have a car and want a more casual day, venture 30 minutes south of Portland to Oregon City to experience both Willamette Falls and the Municipal Elevator. A traditional fishing site where native Americans still harvest Pacific lamprey today, the natural block falls is the largest by volume of water in the Pacific Northwest. Find viewpoints for the falls along Highway 99E and Interstate 205 (milepost 7.5) before the now-defunct paper mill converts into a public space. The 130-foot-municipal elevator that has been connecting the base and upper levels of town since 1955 is one of only four such structures in the world.

🏠 Falls: McLoughlin Blvd., OR 97045; Elevator: 6 Railroad Ave., OR 97045

🔗 www.oregon.com/attractions/willamette-falls

📎 Elevator operates on extended hours from June to October and closes on public holidays.

"Even though it is outside Portland's limits, it is a great excuse to get out of town and take in some Oregon's beauty."

– Keri Elmsly, Second Story

11 Oaks Park

Map Y, P.110

Considered the "Coney Island of the North-west", Oaks Park is the only amusement park currently operating in the city of Portland. The park has been open since 1905 and features go-karts, miniature golf, carnival games, bumper cars, a ferris wheel, and many other rides. If you find yourself in the roller skating rink, make sure to look up as an organ is elevated above the rink floor. While Oregon is mainly synonymous with *The Goonies* (1985), Oaks Park was also featured in the popular film *Free Willy* (1993).

🕐 *Late Mar to mid-Jun: 1200-1900 (Sa-M),
Mid-Jun to mid-Sep: 1200-2100 (Tu-Th), -2200 (F),
-1900 (Su & P.H.)*
💲 *Park: Day pass/pay-as-you-go, Rink: $6.25-7.50,
Skate rentals: $1.75-5.00*
🏠 *7805 SE Oaks Park Way, OR 97202*
📞 *+1 (503) 233 5777* **URL** *www.oakspark.com*

"*I love the colors and energy of the place. You can walk around without paying a dime, so sometimes I just explore and people watch and play arcade games.*"
– Kayla Mattes

12 Mt. Angel Abbey Library
Map Z, P.110

Come for the architecture and stay for the literature. Situated on the grounds of the Mt. Benedict Monastery near the beautiful town of Mt. Angel, this library is one of only two buildings in North America designed by Finnish architect and Artek's founder, Alvar Aalto. Filled with the most entrancing light, the building offers a tranquil and contemplative space where people can explore its famous medieval manuscript collections. You'll need a car to visit this landmark as the library is located approximately one hour south of the Portland city proper.

🕐 Day: 0830-1700 (M-F), 1000-1600 (Sa), 1300-1600 (Su), Evening: 1830-2130 (Su-Th), Summer & PH except state and religious holidays: 0900-1600 (M-F), 1000- (Sa)
🏠 1 Abbey Dr., St Benedict, OR 97373
☎ +1 (503) 845 3303
🌐 mountangelabbey.org/abbey-library

"I fell in love with this place during a photoshoot for Gray Magazine. Try to visit in the earlier hours of the morning or in the late afternoon."
– Arthur Hitchcock

Cultural & Art Spaces

A creative nerve center, land of galleries, weirdness and artistic ventures

"Keep Portland Weird", a common slogan within the city, was originally adopted to promote local business in the area, but has become an unofficial motto for the city, representing its eccentric and atypical character. Portland has found itself at the center of a growing creative population in recent years and is now home to some of the world's leading companies in flourishing industries like apparel, advertising, and technology. These industries have encouraged an influx of innovative talent that helps to shape the city's culture and aspirations, inspiring more people to contribute back to their communities by opening galleries, storefronts, cafes, and even collaborative workspaces like ADX (#22), where local designers, entrepreneurs, and makers bring their ideas to life. A large part of Portland's creative scene centers on the many galleries spread across town. The First Thursday Art Walk, a tradition that has been running since the 1980s, sees many of these galleries hosting open houses for visitors to browse works ranging from sculpture to photography in the Pearl District, Alberta Street, and other areas. Many galleries, including Nationale (#18), provide free beer and wine for art lovers to enjoy during this unique night.

Kat Bauman
Staff writer, Hand-Eye Supply

I use my background in mechanics, self-taught art, and critical theory to find out how things are made and help people get excited about making their own projects happen.

WildCraft Studio School P.035

Annie McLaughlin
Artist

I'm a happy person who likes making things with paint, wood, clay, and fibers. I live in Southeast Portland and am into hot springs and good food with good friends.

Jeremy Pelley & Fritz Mesenbrink, *OMFGCO*

We are the Official Manufacturing Company, aka OMFGCO. We build brands for visionaries. We also like sunsets and long walks on the beach.

Curiosity Club @Hand-Eye Supply P.034

Milk Milk Lemonade P.036

Ryan Bubnis
Illustrator, artist & educator

Bubnis' work explores themes of memory, nostalgia, good vibes, and the human condition. He is also an Assistant Professor at The Pacific Northwest College of Art in Portland, Oregon.

Carl & Sloan P.038

Alex Calvert & Chelsea Spear, *Sincerely Truman*

Calvert and Spear are an unlikely duo with a passion for adventure matched by their love of Portland. At Sincerely Truman, they help people tell their stories to the world.

Emily Counts
Artist & jewelry designer

I create mixed media sculpture with a focus in ceramics, along with designing and producing jewelry in porcelain and bronze for my company St. Eloy.

One Grand Gallery P.037

Nationale P.039

T. Ngu
Jewelry designer

I'm always looking, always seeing, always hearing but I'm not always there. Mom of two pitbull mixes. Love running. Coconut, Belgium fries and Mexican food are my favorite.

Compound Gallery P.042

Katsu Tanaka
Founder, Kiriko & Compound Gallery

I was raised in Japan and schooled in Portland. I exported vintage goods to Japan before opening Compound Gallery. In 2012, I founded Kiriko which goes back to my trading roots.

Alex DeSpain
Illustrator

Alex DeSpain grew up in Oklahoma before moving to Texas and Oregon. He's done contract work for many including Uber. He is the official illustrator for Design Week Portland 2016.

Forest For The Trees P.040

Independent Publishing Resource Center P.043

Kelley Roy
Founder, ADX & Portland Made

Roy has been dedicated to growing Portland's Maker Movement and helping creatives make a living doing what they love. She co-authored *Cartopia: Portland's Food Cart Revolution* in 2010.

The Lincoln Street Kayak & Canoe Museum P.046

David Keltner
Principal & lead designer, Hacker

Formerly a member of Portland's Design Review Commission, Keltner is a devoted protector of Portland's urban character and proponent of sustainable urban development.

Rob Shaw
Director, BENT

Shaw is a superfan who can recite animation stats like a baseball card collector. In 2006 he decided to focus on directing and has been Bent Image Lab's marquee director ever since.

ADX P.044

Hollywood Theatre P.047

13 Curiosity Club
@Hand-Eye Supply

Map C, P.103

Hand-Eye Supply is a go to source for creatives, crafters, and even office supply geeks. Their store contains an array of tools for any project at hand from hacksaws to fountain pens. In addition to the shop, every other Tuesday the shop hosts a speaker series. Their subjects range from astrophysicists waxing poetics about the Milky Way to the relationship between mental health and creative work discussed by photographers and architects, making for an overall excellent stop for to get the one to get the creative tools and inspiration needed.

🕐 1800– (Tu fortnightly), Store: 1100-1800 daily
🏠 427 NW Broadway, OR 97209
📞 +1 (503) 575 9769
URL curiosityclub.handeyesupply.com

"The talks are free and made merrier with food and locally brewed drinks. Creative companies are an unbeatable part of the Portland experience!"

– Kat Bauman, Hand-Eye Supply

14 WildCraft Studio School
Map V, P.109

An art studio and educational center focused on a mixture of craft art and plant medicine, Wildcraft Studio School hosts workshops at their two studios that help students comprehend the connection everything has to nature. Courses last from a day to four weeks, with activities ranging from basket weaving to foraging for mushrooms psychedelic or otherwise. If you're visiting their White Salmon Studio, take a detour and go on a hike at Coyote Wall afterwards for panoramic views that are spectacular no matter what time of year.

🕐 🏠 WSS: 27 Bates Rd., White Salmon, WA 98672; Portland studio: 1830–2130 (M-Th), 1000–1600 (Sa-Su), 601 SE Hawthorne Blvd., OR 97214
📞 +1 (509) 310 3344
🔗 wildcraftstudioschool.com

"The drive out there is beautiful, the workshops are inspiring, and they always include an amazing homemade lunch at the studio."

– Annie McLaughlin

15 Milk Milk Lemonade
Map F, P.105

People who know the playground anthem might be disappointed to find no fudge shops round the corner, but not with the beautiful things lined up at this pleasantly scented place. Home to OLO Fragrance which perfumer Heather Sielaff and her husband launched in 2009, Milk Milk Lemonade carries a hodgepodge of the owner's favorite home goods and, jewelry alongside their products that will gently remind you of the scent from the Pacific Northwest. OLO's fragrances are cruelty-free and hand blended on site.

🕐 1100-1800 (Th-Sa), -1600 (Su)
🏠 1407 SE Belmont St., OR 97214
📞 +1 (503) 970 1173
URL milkmilklemonade.virb.com, olofragrance.com
🖉 Check Instagram/Twitter for up to date hours

"While this isn't a gallery per se, it has some of the best art and curation in the city. Be sure to check their Instagram or call ahead for up to date hours!"

– Jeremy Pelley & Fritz Mesenbrink, OMFGCO

16 One Grand Gallery
Map F, P.105

One Grand Gallery features some of the most diverse programing in the city of Portland. Opened in 2012 by Jordan Chan-Mendez, the gallery plays host to a variety of types of solo and group exhibits to creative agency partnerships, showcasing work from established artists, emerging talent, as well as artist in residence. Past exhibits have focused on a range of subject matters, from dedications to the Notorious B.I.G. to the original Portland International Airport carpet.

🕐 1200–1800 (W–Sa)
🏠 1000 E Burnside St., OR 97233
📞 +1 (971) 266 4919
URL www.onegrandgallery.com

"As both a commercial and fine artist, I appreciate galleries that can successfully blur the line between these two disciplines. One Grand does this flawlessly."
– Ryan Bubnis

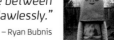

🔴 17 Carl & Sloan
Map R, P.109

Carl & Sloan is a contemporary gallery focusing on new up and coming artists along with well established talent whose subjects encompass culture and critical art theory. Carl & Sloan's index of artists includes; Emily Counts, Hayley Barker, Fay Ray, and many more. Artists themselves and owners, Calvin Ross Carl and Ashley Sloan take over a space inside the Disjecta Contemporary Art Center in Kenton, which is also home to the Portland Biennial, a curator-in-residence program and artists studios. The facility only welcomes the public from Friday to Sunday and might be closed in between shows.

🕐 1200–1700 Su & by appointment
🏠 8371 N Interstate Ave. #1, OR 97217
📞 +1 (360) 608 9746 [URL] www.carlsloan.com

"Bringing a bottle of wine is always a great way to chat and learn about their experiences in the Portland art scene, and their future ambitions for the gallery."

– Alex Calvert & Chelsea Spear, Sincerely Truman

18 Nationale

Map H, P.106

An independently owned art gallery and boutique located in Southeast Portland, Nationale aims to promote new ideas through the lens of culturally diverse art, performances, and goods. Owner and director May Barruel consistently brings in her French sensibility into the collection of art, design objects and publications for sale or display. The gallery currently represents eight dedicated artists in their space and features an anthology of pieces of art from prior exhibitions in their backroom, which are available to purchase.

🕐 1200–1800 (W–M)
🏠 3360 SE Division, OR 97202
📞 +1 (503) 477 9786
URL www.nationale.us

"May has created a very artful and thoughtful space. Make sure to check out the backroom where paintings and sculptures are all displayed salon-style."

– Emily Counts

19 Forest For The Trees

Organized by artist Gage Hamilton, curator Matt Wagner of Hellion Gallery and event producer Tia Vanich, this arts-based nonprofit is committed to bringing fresh art to old walls in the hopes of improving appreciation for creativity in Portland. Each year the week-long event convenes a new group of artists, both local and domestic, to paint murals across the city. Portland-based legends, such as Blaine Fontana, Hamilton himself, and the likes of INSA, have participated since the project kicked off in 2013. While everyone can watch creative visions unfold during the day, the fun continues with music, artists sharing sections and bike tours at night and after the event.

🕐 Mid-August
URL www.forestforthetreesnw.com

"*The best way to experience Portland and visit the local neighborhoods is by biking to see each mural.*"
– T. Ngu

20 Compound Gallery
Map C, P.103

With its doors opening in 2002, Compound Gallery is one of Portland's first shops to carry streetwear. With an up-to-date awareness of the best in urban art and design, Japanese and American pop culture floods the store and its selection of local brands such as Jaefields, industry giants like Stüssy, vintage goods, design magazines and sneakers. Glass cases on the ground floor display vinyl toys that owner Katsu Tanaka sourced mostly from Japan with a collection of super rare sneakers all displayed as if they were artifacts. Each Thursday the upper level of Compound opens a month long show featuring a collection of art from local artists and sometimes group exhibitions.

🕐 1100-1900 (M-Sa), 1200-1800 (Su)
🏠 107 NW 5th Ave., OR 97209   📞 +1 (503) 796 2733
URL compoundgallery.com

"It's more about street culture and urban art, than fine art. Stop in for a cookie at the front register!"

– Katsu Tanaka, Kiriko & Compound Gallery

21 Independent Publishing Resource Center

Map A, P.102

If you've dreamed of making zines dedicated to your exquisite drawings, food experience or travelogue then the Independent Publishing Resource Center has you covered. With an affordable membership you'll receive access to a computer lab with design suites, a letterpress studio, bookbinding supplies, screen printing studio, and more. The center provides educational workshops and formal certificate programs on topics relating to publishing, writing and artwork any ambitious self-publisher would find enlightening.

🕐 1200–2100 (Su–F), –1800 (Sa)
🏠 1001 SE Division St., OR 97202
📞 +1 (503) 827 0249 **URL** www.iprc.org

"It's a gateway experience. Just have fun! It's a great creative space and the equipment puts the power of production in your hands."

– Alex DeSpain

22 ADX
Map F, P.105

Started as a collaborative makerspace for designers, entrepreneurs and hobbyists, ADX has become a central hub for local makers to grow their businesses and build relationships within Portland's maker community. Inside you'll find metal shop, 3D printers, laser cutter, wood shop, a full library of tools, sewing machines, and much more. All of which is available for members to create anything their hearts desire and imaginations can conjure. Three times a week ADX offers public tours to allow guests to survey the facility while instructional courses demonstrate tools and mastery on different skill levels.

🕐 0900–2200 (M–F), –2100 (Sa–Su)
🏠 417 SE 11th Ave., OR 97214
📞 +1 (503) 915 4342
URL adxportland.com

"If you plan in advance you can even sign up for a class or two, work alongside local makers and find out what makes these entrepreneurs tick."

– Kelley Roy, ADX & Portland Made

23 The Lincoln Street Kayak & Canoe Museum

Map K, P.107

With a keen passion in the study and practice of original Greenlandic watercraft, Harvey Golden is a scholarly researcher, boat-builder extraordinaire and a published author, having written the history of traditional kayaks in both Greenland and Alaska. His studies involve hand-crafting replica kayaks and canoes, which one can find at this private museum, demonstrating varying uses and incredible artistry from their design to joinery methods. Read the guide online and make full use of the two hours to take in its growing collection!

🕐 1700-1900 (W)
🏠 5340 SE Lincoln St., OR 97215 📞 +1 (503) 234 0264
URL www.traditionalkayaks.com/museum.html

"I love that it's solely dedicated to replicating traditional indigenous water vessels. Plan your trip! It only opens two hours per week, which is so Portland."

– David Keltner, Hacker

# 24 Hollywood Theatre
Map J, P.107

The Hollywood Theatre is at once a traditional movie space and a nonprofit that provides film production education programs for teenagers. Open since 1926, the theatre has maintained their original interior, boasting the only functional 70mm projector in the state of Oregon and even a renovated marquee crafted based on their original one. If you're bored of the traditional movie-going experience, attend one of Hollywood's themed nights such as Hecklevision where audience members can text their trash talk about bad films to be displayed directly on screen while the movie is playing.

🕐 Open 30 minutes prior to the first showing
💲 $12/9/7/6 🏠 4122 NE Sandy Blvd., OR 97212
📞 +1 (503) 281 4215 🌐 hollywoodtheatre.org

"There's no reason to see the most recent blockbuster here. You want the cult, fringe and art films. If they have 'Kung Fu Theater' while you're in town, GO!"
– Rob Shaw, BENT

Markets & Shops

Artisanal wears, the freshest possible produce, furniture
and records galore

The bountiful shops and marketplaces scattered across Portland
can be hard to find, but they're overflowing with accessories for
any lifestyle. From high-end pieces to vintage treasures passed
down from who-knows-where, stores in the city – especially clothing boutiques – never fail to surprise shoppers. While most local
designers and farmers sell their products exclusively at their own
stores, some of the more well-known products also appear in local
businesses, such as Tanner Goods for leather products (*www.tan-
nergoods.com*) and Olympic Provisions for housemaid charcuterie
(*www.olympiaprovisions.com*). You can find a cluster of these
shops – carrying selvage denim, artisanal chocolate, and more – at
the downtown shopping arcade Union Way (*1022 W. Burnside St., OR
97209*) and alongside Mississippi Street, which is also home to the
record digger's paradise Beacon Sound (*www.wearebeaconsound.
com*), nifty design studios, and several incredible book and comic
shops. Beyond clothing and bookstores, remarkable locally-de-
signed and produced furniture businesses pepper the city, creating
functional pieces that double as one-off works of art.

Delaney Allen
Artist

Delaney Allen received his MFA from Pacific Northwest College of Art in 2010. He is represented in by Nationale Gallery and has published four books through Publication Studio in Portland.

Reading
Frenzy
P.053

Kate Bingaman-Burt
Illustrator & educator

I have been living in and loving Portland since 2008. My work orbits around the objects in our lives: the things we buy and discard.

Casey Keasler
Founder, Casework

My creative studio focuses on environments and how they are experienced. Our goal is to understand a client's needs and ideas, then translate them into an experience.

Publication
Studio
P.052

The
Good Mod
P.054

Worn Path
P.057

Taralyn Thuot
Creative director, Wildfang

Formally a Nike vet with ten years of experience in marketing, experience design, and concept direction, I now channel my creative energy into building a home for the modern Tomboy.

Pure Bathing Culture
Band

We're Daniel and Sarah. We moved here from New York City in 2011. It's wonderful to see so much of the world as touring musicians, it always feels just right to come home to Portland.

Jeff Luker
Photographer

When not shooting fashion or advertising campaigns, I will be out exploring all the natural wonders the Pacific Northwest has to offer.

Wildfang
P.056

Clinton Street
Record &
Stereo
P.058

Ryan Unruh & Matt Jones
Creative duo

When not creating, still life photographer Unruh would spend time with his wife and dogs. If sleep wasn't required to survive, product stylist Jones would never stop dinking around.

Beam & Anchor
P.060

Ryan Donohoe
Furniture designer & craftsman

I transitioned from architecture to furniture to have more autonomy and control over the final product and to spend more time building and less time on the computer. I love my job.

Jessica Helgerson
Jessica Helgerson Interior Design

I am the principal of a small, creative interior design firm, with one foot happily and firmly rooted in Portland and the other dipping into the other amazing places this planet has to offer.

2nd Avenue Records
P.059

Hippo Hardware & Trading Co
P.062

Devon Burt
VP Apparel Innovation Design, Nike

I've been around the world and Portland, where I was born, is by far one of my favorite cities. It's accessible and is growing into a wonderful creative city with its own aesthetic.

Palace
P.064

Rather Severe
Creative duo

Rather Severe is artists Jon Stommel and Travis Czekalski. They paint murals and illustrate imagery exploring themes of dream logic, absurdism, and humorous abstraction.

Tim Blanchard
Stylist

Born and raised from this amazing city, I love music, being active and I appreciate genuine people with good conversation. Experiencing new things everyday is my goal.

Really Good Stuff
P.063

Portland Farmers Market @PSU
P.065

25 Publication Studio
Map C, P.103

Since its formation in 2009, Publication Studio has been shifting the paradigm of how people look at the publishing economy globally. Run by Patricia No and Antonia Pinter, the Portland shop continues to co-create original works with artists, photographers, authors and the like, and only print and bind books in the shop's front as orders arrive to ensure all books produced have a home. Check for their collaborative events, book launch, and artists talks that irregularly happen at their space or other venues, such as the annual Publication Fair held at Ace Hotel.

🕐 1100-1700 (M-F)
🏠 717 SW Ankeny St., OR 97205
📞 +1 (503) 360 4702
f Publication Studio Portland, Ore.
URL www.publicationstudio.biz

"During the last five years I've seen their roster of books grow substantially with a wide variety of projects. Visit with the idea of staying for a while."
– Delaney Allen

26 Reading Frenzy
Map M, P.108

The hysteria for literature began in 1994 when Reading Frenzy opened its doors in Portland. Having since confronted the mainstream of selling books around politics and current affairs, the independently-run shop and gallery space has managed to publicize arts and culture and grown to become a cult classic among the bibliophile community. Its publishing offshoot Show & Tell Press is another attempt that owner Chloe Eudaly made to bring out-of-print titles to life. Its extensive selection of zines, small press, and self-published work can take hours to explore it all.

🕐 1100-1900 (M-Sa), 1200-1700 (Su)
🏠 3628 N Mississippi Ave., OR 97227
📞 +1 (971) 271 8044   URL www.readingfrenzy.com

"Zine lovers rejoice. Reading Frenzy is here for you. The incredible Craphound is also published by Show & Tell Press."

– Kate Bingaman-Burt

27 The Good Mod

Map C, P.102

Nestled on the fourth floor of an unassuming warehouse in the Pearl district, The Good Mod is a furniture and design dreamland filled with the most expertly crafted and restored home goods you've ever laid your eyes on. The showroom displays one of the largest collections of mid-century and Danish modern furniture in the nation. While the prices match the quality of the work, it is free to visit the space. Ask for a workshop tour and challenge the staff to a game of ping pong on one of their signature tables.

🕐 1100–1800 daily
🏠 4th Floor, 1313 W Burnside St., OR 97209
📞 +1 (503) 206 6919
🔗 www.thegoodmod.com

"Great spot to see design favorites and learn about lesser known designers. It doesn't stop there, the space is perfect for your next photo shoot."

– Casey Keasler, Casework

28 Wildfang

Map F, P.105

Taking its name from the German word for tomboy, Wildfang is a one-stop shop for masculine clothing and accessories with a feminine edge. Following an androgynous movement in the fashion industry, founders and Nike alum Emma Mcilroy and Julia Parsley, later joined by creative director Taralyn Thuot, lead the voice with many brands and exclusive collaborations that cater to the wardrobe of girls who prefer wingtips to ballerinas, manly silhouettes to figure-flattering cuts, and jewels that do more than sparkle. Fort Wildfang in Southeast is its original store and where the brains work.

🕐 Fort: 1200–1800 daily, West: 1100–1900 (Su–Th), 1000–2000 (F–Sa)
🏠 Fort: 1230 SE Grand Ave., OR 97214, West: 404 SW 10th Ave., OR 97205
📞 Fort: +1 (503) 208 3631, West: +1 (503) 964 6746
URL www.wildfang.com

"Be sure to make your mark on their giant carving wall alongside the likes of Janelle Monáe, Chvrches, Brittney Griner and Tegan and Sara."

– Taralyn Thuot, Wildfang

29 Worn Path

Map M, P.108

Succeeding the well known Mississippi Records'
store that since moved, this little outdoors-
focused shop houses products that bring
aesthetics and function together to help you
enjoy Portland's open air. Its look and feel is
inspired by great American gift shops that exist
in abundance around the country but with Portland's staple modern vintage appeal. Many of
Oregon's local outdoors enthusiast apparel and
gear are stocked here along with books, skate
decks, prints, camping supplies and much more.

🕐 1100–1900 (M–Tu, Th–Sa), –1800 (Su)
🏠 4007 N Mississippi Ave., OR 97227
📞 +1 (503) 208 6156   f WORN PATH
URL www.worn-path.com

*"The taste level of Niles Armstrong, the owner, is
amazing. They also print their own line of tees, hats and
tote bags with rad designs that change fairly often."*

– Jeff Luker

30 Clinton Street Record & Stereo

Map H, P.106

The quality of new and used records and selection of stereo equipment stocked in Clinton Street's storefront more than make up for what this shop lacks in space. The owner, Jared White, is extremely knowledgable and has laser sharp recommendations based on preferences described to him. He also moonlights as DJ Maxx Bass after hours at clubs and bars such as Dig A Pony and The Liquor Store. When it's not raining, dig through its amazing dollar bin out front. You might come up with something you would want to listen to.

🕐 1300–1900 daily
🏠 2510 SE Clinton St., OR 97202
📞 +1 (503) 235 5323
URL clintonstreetrecordandstereo.com

"There are too many good record stores here to pick just one, so we won't. In NE our favorite is Beacon Sound, which is larger and just as well curated."

– Pure Bathing Culture

31 2nd Avenue Records

Map C, P.103

Easily an unmissable shop for anyone who enjoys music and record digging with a good price point to match, 2nd Avenue Records at first glance resembles that of a busy trade show booth, with hundreds of decade-old band T-shirts suspended from the ceilings. Every surface is covered either by posters or stickers leaving very little area for the eye to rest freely. The downtown shop's somewhat cluttered collection of records covers many genres including punk, metal, reggae, and hip hop, coupled with a wonderful bevy of secondhand CDs and LPs.

🕐 1100–2000 (M–F), 1000– (Sa), 1200–1800 (Su)
🏠 400 SW 2nd Ave., OR 97204
📞 +1 (503) 222 3783   f 2nd Avenue Records
URL www.2ndavenuerecords.com

"They have a staggering amount of vinyl for every taste. Plan to spend more time than you think you'll need."

– Ryan Unruh & Matt Jones

32 Beam & Anchor

Map M, P.108

Tucked away in northeast industrial Portland, Beam & Anchor comprises a fully functional retail front and a large studio space oozing a community vibe. Enter the 7,000-square-foot warehouse facing the train yard by the river and find yourself circled by upholstered furniture, jewelry, organic fragrance, bags and textiles, many of which are sourced locally or crafted by designers and artists working upstairs. Check instagram for regular updates as spouses and founders Jocelyn and Robert Rahm often host themed dinners, workshops and open studios throughout the year.

🕐 1100-1800 (M-Sa), 1200-1700 (Su)
🏠 2710 N Interstate Ave., OR 97227
📞 +1 (503) 367 3230 URL beamandanchor.com

"I love Beam & Anchor for being a perfect reflection of the Portland aesthetic and the Portland crafts scene."

– Jessica Helgerson

33 Hippo Hardware & Trading Co
Map F, P.105

More than just a hardware store, Hippo
Hardware is a portal into Portland's past by
way of secondhand soccer ball, painted light
fixtures and knick knacks saved from torn
down homes. Located on the corner of East
Burnside and SE 11th Ave, the mystical three
floor 30,000-square-foot warehouse has every
square inch filled with all that you've dreamed
about having in your home, from clawfoot
bathtubs filled with lifesized Hippopotamus
stuffed toys to an assortment of door knobs
and toilets. Come for the hardware. Leave with
a piece of Pacific Northwest history.

🕐 1000-1700 (M-Th), -1800 (F-Sa), 1200-1700 (Su)
🏠 1040 E Burnside St., OR 97214
📞 +1 (503) 231 1444 🔗 www.hippohardware.com

*"Try and find something nice and small like a cool
knocker for the front door or an antique doorknob
that fit in luggage better than a new chandelier."*
– Ryan Donohoe

34 Really Good Stuff
Map F, P.105

A vintage store filled with trinkets and doodads crammed into a dusty attic-like environment in Southeast Portland. They've got everything that justifies the official store motto "Life's necessary nonessentials," from a claw machine, in case you needed one for your arcade, to an impressive collection of PEZ dispensers. Rumor has it that all television shows and films shot in Portland source their props from this shop. On Mondays, if you arrive at the right time, you'll find free homemade cookies.

🕑 1100-1900 daily
🏠 1322 SE Hawthorne Blvd., OR 97214
📞 +1 (503) 238 1838

"I love finding things that no one else has and Really Good Stuff is closer to going through your grandparents attic than anything else. Watch out for the cat."

– Devon Burt, Nike

35 Palace
Map G, P.106

Eclectic and offbeat, and perhaps color-coordinated, Palace carries a great selection of vintage clothing and products for men and women curated by its owner Charlotte Wenzel inspired by the love of thrifting. Her focus is unisex items that contain natural fabrics in their assembly. The shop also sells new modern products setting them next to the vintage items, along with jewelry, apothecary and home accessories. For a special surprise, swing by the space on any Monday to receive 15% off all items in the shop.

🕐 1100-1900 daily
🏠 2205 E Burnside St., OR 97214
📞 +1 (503) 517 0123
URL palacestore.tumblr.com

"I love Palace because of the variety of items the store is able to sell and mix together. Ask about local designers carried at the shop!"

– Tim Blanchard

36 Portland Farmers Market @PSU
Map E, P.104

Oregon is known for its love for organic, environmentally conscious agriculturists and product vendors, and it wouldn't be Portland without a local, direct to the customer, farmers market. Once a week, year round, more than 150 vendors convene in the park blocks of Portland State University to share and sell their items, featuring everything from fresh pastured hen and duck eggs to hand-crafted small-batched kimchi. Local farmers produce and meats can also be found circulating around some of the acclaimed Portland cuisine, which proves the market's quality.

🕐 Sa: 0830-1400 (Mar-Oct), 0900- (Nov-Feb)
🏠 SW Park & SW Montgomery, OR 97201
URL www.portlandfarmersmarket.org/our-markets/psu

"Highly recommend Spring Hill Organic Farm for amazing produce."
– Rather Severe

Restaurants & Cafés

Wild fusion food, unique adaptations and premier chefs

Portland offers thousand of tastes in a league of their own. Cuisines of every type can be found throughout the entire city, with restaurants and cafés doing wonders for the city's economy while providing a top-notch spread of coffee shops, bars, and sit-down dining spots. Portland restaurants feature a world of creative adaptations and fusions of ethnic cuisines for taste buds to explore. Ingredients used are frequently authentic to the Northwest, as they're often sourced directly from local farmers and producers no more than a few hours away. Notorious for their love of brunching, Portlanders are no strangers to enduring long lines for late-morning meals. One of these popular morning destinations, Sweedeedee (#46), provides breakfast treats baked in-house. If you're not in a hurry, take the time to immerse yourself in the stylish interiors of breakfast spots such as the Scandinavian-inspired Broder Nord (*www.broderpdx. com*), or head for the punchy American options at Roost (*roostpdx. com*). Many dining options the city are specially themed to entice customers and enhance their experiences. Whether you're looking for a carefully-brewed and expertly presented espresso, or chicken wings marinated in fish sauce with origins in Southeast Asia, Portland's wide range of food choices will never disappoint.

The Vera Firm
Creative agency

The Vera Firm consists of Vincent Magee, Nick Woolley and Anthony Taylor. We focus on branding, photography, film, music, manufacturing products and curate for pop up events.

Oso Market + Bar
P.071

Matt Hayes
Filmmaker & editor

The core battery that keeps people making and sharing genuinely interesting work here is far from fading. While I've only been a Portlander for four years, I'm proud to call this place home.

Adam Friedman
Visual artist

Based in Portland, OR, I just opened a new solo exhibition at Mirus Gallery in SF, CA called "Into the Aether."

Stumptown Coffee Roasters
P.070

Toro Bravo
P.072

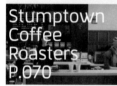

Andy Luce
Designer, typographer & letterer

Specializing in branding, I pursue a tangible world in digital spaces. When not designing, I can be found adventuring outside in nature with his wife, Liz.

Angel Face
P.075

Andee Hess
Owner, Osmose Design

I am the principal designer of Osmose, a highly collaborative practice that tells stories through installations and customized furnishings for commercial and residential environments.

Josh Kenyon & Colby Nichols, *Jolby & Friends*

We are the co-founders and creative directors of Jolby & Friends. We started the studio in 2010, and now work with a team dedicated to creating the best collaborative work possible.

Navarre
P.074

Langbaan
P.076

Johnny Le
Founder & curator, Hideout

Also a filmmaker and photographer, I contribute to *Hypebeast* and *Highsnobiety*. Hideout connects art and nightclub experiences with businesses in Portland, LA and Vancouver.

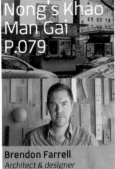

Nong's Khao
Man Gai
P.079

Brendon Farrell
Architect & designer

I am a licensed architect. Born and raised in Southern Oregon, I design and build architecture projects, furniture, educational products, lighting fixtures and mobile dwelling units.

Escape Collective
Set & product design group

We are a group of designers, engineers, builders and sewers and, overall, creatives. Friends before business partners, we are a one-stop-shop for solutions of your wildest dreams.

Phở Lê
P.078

Tidbit
Food Farm &
Garden
P.080

Bijan Berahimi
Graphic designer

While at CalArts, I founded journal FISK, which later became a gallery, and the annual CalArts Print Fair. He is an instigator for the development and integration of design in his community.

P's & Q's
Market
P.082

Davis Priestley
Film & photo producer

I run a production company and consultancy called Priestley & Co. We work in film, interactive and emerging storytelling, and stills production.

Hovercraft
Design studio

Hovercraft think, design & create for brands and products. New Mexico-native Ryan Haaland co-founded the studio with Zack Teachout in 2009, and has lived in Portland for four years.

Sweedeedee
P.081

Caffe Mingo
P.083

37 Stumptown Coffee Roasters
Map C, P.103

Stumptown Coffee has become a principal roaster in the Northeast of the U.S. An array of signature coffee blends and artisanal approach to the coffee business has given Stumptown credit within the states for being a part of a coffee movement that strives to create high quality artisanal coffee. Stumptown has several locations in Portland, one of which is located within the busy Ace Hotel with a comfortable lounge area attracting locals and visitors alike. Their popular individually bottled cold brew coffee is distributed in retailers and marketplaces across the country.

🕑 0600-1900 (M-F), 0700- (Sa-Su)
🏠 Downtown: 128 SW 3rd Ave., OR 97204
📞 +1 (855) 711 3385 URL www.stumptowncoffee.com

"Visit the downtown location and ask for Ripley Snell. If he is around, mention you'd like to try one of his secret concoctions!"

– The Vera Firm

38 Oso Market + Bar
Map F, P.105

A bar with esteemed mixologists to the left, a wall of wines, cooking oils, local teas and chocolates to the right, and endless Spanish- and French-inspired options for your stomach. Bag a seat at the bar so that you can strike up a conversation with the staff and ask them to create their best concoctions. Washing down their Charcuterie Desayuno and Romesco Montadito with El Guano (a vodka, madeira, combier, bitters and lemon topped with soda elixir) for brunch will lift you to cloud nine.

🕐 1100–2200 (Tu-Th), –2300 (F), 1000– (Sa), –2100 (Su)
🏠 726 SE Grand Ave., OR 97214
📞 +1 (503) 232 6400
URL osomarket.com
🖉 Reservations required for parties of 6 or more

"If there's one thing I love about Oso Market, it's their attention to detail. Ask the staff what they're really excited to try that week - you won't be disappointed."

– Matt Hayes

39 Toro Bravo
Map P, P.108

A Spanish tapas-inspired restaurant owned by serial restaurateur chef John Gorham, the mastermind behind local favorites Tasty N Alder and Tasty N Sons, Toro Bravo is a favorite haunt of lovebirds and small parties of friends. Limiting reservations to groups of seven or more means you'd better arrive before 6pm or expect a wait for up to two hours. Once settled in, go straight for Clam Cataplana for starters and Stuffed Piquillo Peppers for entrée. Or, trust the chef by getting their revered tasting menu. Buen provecho!

🕐 1700–2200 (Su–Th), –2300 (F–Sa)
🏠 120 NE Russell St., OR 97212
🕐 +1 (503) 281 4464
URL www.torobravopdx.com
🔗 Reservations for parties of 7–14 only (Su–Th)

"Best tapas restaurant I've ever been to, hands down. Get there early or hit the bar upstairs for some nice cocktails while you wait."

– Adam Friedman

40 Navarre

Map G, P.106

A romantic, candle-lit environment perfect for a date but delicious enough to go on your own, Navarre serves small and large plates perfect for sharing. Simplify your life by selecting the "We Choose" option where you'll receive ten plates hand selected by the chef and prepared with what's freshly delivered from their urban community farm that week. Don't forget to pair their food with wine sourced throughout Europe. The trout baked in parchment is the best item on the menu. No reservations for groups of less than six, so get there before the brunch rush.

🕐 1630–2230 (M–Th), –2330 (F), 0930–2330 (Sa),
–2230 (Su) 🏠 10 NE 28th Ave., OR 97232
📞 +1 (503) 232 3555 URL www.navarreportland.com

"Dinner service is lovely, but the true hidden gem is their weekend brunch! Be sure to order bread, salted butter and jam to share. It's to die for (I don't say that lightly)."
– Andy Luce

41 Angel Face

Map G, P.106

This mystery bar is decorated with pink walls, adorned by blue flowers and equipped with no drink menu. Explore the depths of your mind and palate to explain to the barkeeps what you're in the mood for and they'll add notes to the groundwork of your liquid composition to craft a masterful symphony in a glass. Giovanna Parolari and John Taboada, the masterminds behind Navarre (#40) are also responsible for this watering hole. The beauty in this bar is that it expands your knowledge of spirits by challenging the norms of you drink traditions. Come explore new alcoholic horizons!

🕐 1700-0000 (Su–Th), -0100 (F-Sa)
🏠 14 NE 28th Ave., OR 97232   📞 +1 (503) 239 3804
🔗 www.angelfaceportland.com
🔗 Walk-ins only

"I try not to go here too often, because I really want it to stay perfect forever. Trust the bartenders. Also, order the fish board, half or whole."

– Andee Hess

42 Langbaan
Map G, P.106

If you're walking on SE 28th Street you might miss this delightful Thai restaurant, as there's no signage. Hidden within the confines of PaaDee, Langbaan opened its doors in 2014 with a splash, making it to the semifinals of the Best New Restaurant category for a James Beard award in 2015. Armed with a seasonal tasting menu and only 24 seats, count your lucky stars if you can snag a reservation. It's worth the wait. Our taste buds can attest to this.

🕐 Weekly seatings: 1800, 2045 (Th–Sa), 1730, 2015 (Su)
🏠 6 SE 28th Ave., OR 97214
📞 +1 (971) 344 2564
URL langbaanpdx.com
🖇 Reservations recommended

"Love their seasonal Thai tasting menu. It's one of the best food experiences you can get in Portland."

– Josh Kenyon & Colby Nichols, Jolby & Friends

43 Phở Lê
Map T, P.109

Located in the Fishers Landing Marketplace shopping center just north of the Columbia River, this family-owned restaurant is a gem that's been serving heavenly Vietnamese comfort food since 1991. While egg rolls and phở are the traditional fan favorites, you can't go wrong with tái (sliced beef sirloin steak) and mì xào dòn, featuring crispy fried egg noodle cake topped with vegetable stir fry and meat of your choice. Food lover with an unquenchable stomach can request to size up their dish for a dime.

🕐 1100-2030 (M-Th), -2100 (F-Sa), -2000 (Su)
🏠 2100 SE 164th Ave., D109, Vancouver, WA 98683
📞 +1 (360) 892 8484
URL pho-le.com

"If you're really hungry, order Chả giò (crispy egg rolls)."
– Johnny Le

44 Nong's Khao Man Gai
Map F, P.105

Nong Poonsukwattana's famous "khao man gai" is a well versed take on the popular Hainanese chicken rice. Noted for her house made Thai sauce that blends the perfect amount of spice, Nong's establishment began as a dream in a compact cart that served simply one delicious dish on Alder Street, and has now grown into a thriving Portland attraction at three locations. The original location still hands out only her flavorful chicken and rice in butcher paper wrap as she remembers from her childhood. Her PSU and Ankeny menu extends to include vegetarian options and cocktails.

🕐 Alder: 1000–1600 or sold out (M–F), PSU: 1100–(M–F), Ankeny: 1100–2100 daily

🏠 Alder: SW 10 & Alder St., OR 97205; PSU: SW 4th & 411 SW College St., OR 97201; Ankeny: 609 SE Ankeny St., Suite C, OR 97214

📞 Alder: +1 (971) 255 3480; PSU: +1 (971) 255 3480; Ankeny: +1 (503) 740 2907

URL khaomangai.com 🖉 Cash only

"Great food, simple atmosphere."

– Brendon Farrell

45 Tidbit Food, Farm & Garden
Map H, P.106

Not your traditional cart pod, Tidbit offers a wide array of food styles and mixes in apparel, a florist, and more. With roughly 15,000 square-foot to play with, 24 carts call this space home so you may need a few visits to get through the full gamut of experiences. The pod is outdoors so it's ideal for sunny days and cool evenings by the fire pit. Two standouts are Namu, a Korean/Hawaiian fusion noted for

their Aloha Bowl, and The Doghouse PDX for their "1 Night in Bangkok" burger, with candied bacon, peanut butter, and samba chili sauce.

🕐 General hours: 1000–2200
🏠 SE 28th Pl. & Division St., OR 97202
✉ tidbitfood@gmail.com
📘 Tidbit Food Farm and Garden

"Having six members all with wildly different taste, we can come here and be satisfied. If you are going for dinner, get there early."

– Escape Collective

46 Sweedeedee

Map O, P.108

For those of us who are constantly battling inner demons in choosing between a sweet or savory brunch, Sweedeedee makes it simple to have the best of both worlds. An array of pieces baked in-house, get the salted honey, stare longingly at you at the ordering counter, allowing you to select the breakfast plate (baked eggs, bacon, toast, salad, cheese, and fruit) without feeling guilty. If there's a wait, which there usually is, walk around the corner to Mississippi Records to spend some time digging through music.

🕐 0800–1500 (M–Sa), –1400 (Su)
🏠 5202 N Albina Ave., OR 97217
📞 +1 (503) 946 8087
URL www.sweedeedee.com

"Can't go wrong with Sweedeedee Breakfast Blate, soo good. Everything they do is tasty, especially their bread and other pastry treats. Good portions, great staff."

– Bijan Berahimi

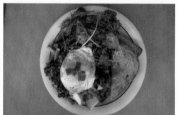

47 P's & Q's Market

Map N, P.108

A hybrid corner store, which stocks a well-curated selection of local goods from fresh produce to milk priced lower than larger grocery stores, P's & Q's also doubles as a restaurant successfully funded by a Kickstarter campaign. Located in Woodlawn, away from the over-saturated restaurant rows further south on the east side of Portland, the store has helped provide the neighborhood, where dining options are scarce, a new and refreshing local option for food. Get the bacon and brisket hash, which comes with a fried egg, kale, sweet potato, apple, salad, and toast, hands down the most popular item on the brunch menu.

🕐 1100-2100 (M-F), 0900- (Sa-Su)
🏠 1301 NE Dekum St., OR 97211
📞 +1 (503) 894 8979   URL www.psandqsmarket.com

"This is the place for the perfect sleepy mid-morning breakfast. Beat the weekend rush and get there within an hour of opening."
– Davis Priestley

48 Caffe Mingo
Map D, P.104

Caffe Mingo claims to have simple Italian cooking but your palate will judge for you. Upon entering the restaurant you'll find a warm vibe immediately and have a clear view into the kitchen from almost anywhere you're seated. The sugo of beef braised in Chianti and espresso with penne pasta is the oldest item on the menu, having been a mainstay since the restaurant opened in 1991. If you're starving, skip the apps and go directly to the mains. And if you're in luck, the brined-and-pan roasted pork chop with creamy polenta, grilled rapini, and mustard pan sauce.

🕐 1700–2200 (M–Sa), 1630–2130 (Su)
🏠 807 NW 21st Ave., OR 97209
📞 +1 (503) 226 4646   f Caffe Mingo
URL caffemingonw.com

"Do yourself a favor and just get the sugo beef penne. They make the best Italian food I've had since living in Italy. Simple as that."

– Hovercraft

Nightlife

Specialty cocktails, craft beer and outlandish nights

In Portland, the nights are as vibrant and energetic as the days. With strong scenes in everything from metal to indie folk, the city's incredible musical diversity bleeds even into the electronic music scene, inspiring incredible parties as well as easy listening at an abundance of bars, lounges, and night clubs. Off-the-wall musicians, DJs and partygoers are drawn by Portland's inexhaustible after-dark culture, and many local musicians find themselves sought after by venues inviting them to share the stage with well-known headliners. One of the first venues of its kind to open in the city, The Crystal Ballroom (*www.crystalballroompdx.com*) held shows by R&B and psychedelic acts in the 1960s and '70s and is now known in part for its unique "floating" floor. Aside from the bar and music scenes, there are also offerings of oddities that range from late night dessert cafés set in ordinary-looking two story homes to classic arcades such as Ground Kontrol (#53) in Old Town. Filled with vintage video games and pinball machines, it also features one of the most dynamic interiors you'll find outside of a nightclub. Make your nights memorable with the help of vast menus of speciality cocktails and even longer lists of microbrew beer, all while exploring the wide spread of adventurous environments these late-night destinations have to provide.

Ibeth Hernandez
Co-founder, Chapters Alumni

A native Portlander, I have been curating music events with my business partner Jacob Robertson since 2010. We're proud to consistently bring the best acts in hip-hop to our region.

Roseland Theater
P.088

Holocene
P.089

Dan Vidmar aka Shy Girls
Singer-songwriter & producer

I've been living here for about six years (a Pennsylvania transplant). My Portland is a miniature Mecca of art, music, DJ, and DIY culture. There's no better place to come home to than Portland.

Martha Grant
Animator & filmmaker

Grant moved to Portland in 2010 to work at LAIKA. After three films there, she decided to retire in her 20s. Now, she animates anything she can to keep away from having to move to LA.

CC Slaughters
P.090

Donovan Edwards
Cultural engineer, Ace Hotel PDX

I am a queer artist and musician. I thrive and am happiest when I exist in free-form creative environments or spaces. Yoga in the AM. Gym in the PM. Posivibes all day.

Lovecraft Bar
P.091

Ground Kontrol
P.092

Mako Miyamoto aka Neon Werewolf

I am a photographer, filmmaker and creative director working at a small design shop in SE Portland.

Kayla Hoppins
Brand experience coordinator

I curate Industry's culture and help produce its flagship events. I'm a Pacific Northwest native and I've been here in Portland for nearly a decade. I'm into style, vinyl, and houseplants.

Goodfoot Pub & Lounge
P.094

The Pressure
Creative studio

We work through whatever comes our way that make sense of it with our energy. Our clients include Nickelodeon, Wired Magazine, Nike, the New York Times, and Kanye West.

Wake The Town @The Liquor Store
P.096

Reva Maureen DeVito
Musician

I am a recording artist and vocalist on HW&W Recordings. I was born and raised in the greater Portland area and continue to represent RIP CITY with gusto. Patti Smith is my hero.

Jason Sturgill
Illustrator & educator

I grew up in a small town nearby and have lived in Portland since 1999. I have worked for several businesses started in Portland, e.g. Nike, Laika, Wieden+Kennedy, Dark Horse Comics and Poler.

White Owl Social Club
P.095

Likewise
P.097

Ryan J. Bush
Filmmaker

I spend a lot of time shooting photos and making weird animated gifs. I watch too many movies and cartoons, and I play lots of video games. I currently live in Northwest Portland.

Bula Kava House
P.099

Kyle Banuelos
Founder, Stublisher Inc.

Stublisher's work is a reflection Banuelo's fascination and exploration of technology, objects and spaces interact and bring people together around shared interests and experiences.

Holly Andres
Photographer

I'm a fine art and commercial photographer. I travel often but love returning home to Portland where I live a rich and resourceful creative life with my two beautiful Siamese cats.

Le Happy
P.098

Stargazing @Mount Tabor Park
P.100

49 **The Roseland Theater**
Map C, P.103

Part of Oregon's largest concert company, The Roseland Theater has had legendary headlining performances during its history such as Ray Charles, Grateful Dead, Bob Dylan, Prince, and the list goes on. The theater features a standing-room only main floor which holds 1400 people at maximum capacity and an upper balcony with seats. There is also a renovated lower level called Peter's Room with a second stage for smaller acts. The venue continues to host Portland's largest visiting multigenerational and multi genre concerts every night of the week.

🕐 💲 *Opening hours/showtime vary with events*
🏠 *8 NW 6th Ave., OR 97209*
📞 *info@roselandpdx.com*
🔗 *roselandpdx.com*

"Cash only venue. If you're over 21, the best place to watch shows from is the balcony so make your way up there before it gets packed!"

– Ibeth Hernandez, Chapters Alumni

50 Holocene

Map F, P.105

A once automobile repair warehouse turned into large packed lively dance floors with a large frequently understaffed bar, Holocene is known for hosting some of Portland's well known parties along with music events like MUSICFESTNW and Red bull Sound Select. Some say that Holocene is the number-one spot in Portland for deep house music although the range of genres the venue has been known to display is vast. The dim to no lighting is perfect for their visuals and light shows during acts. Their bar provides space to comfortably stand or sit to enjoy the show along with craft beer and classic cocktails.

🕐 2030 till late (W-Th), 2100- (F-Sa) or subject to programs 💲 Price varies with programs
🏠 1001 SE Morrison St., OR 97214
📞 +1 (503) 239 7639 URL holocene.org
🔗 21+ unless otherwise noted

"A night at Holocene is the quickest way to get to know some true Portlanders at a very 'Portland' place."

– Dan Vidmar aka Shy Girls

51 CC Slaughters
Map C, P.103

Beside the second largest collection of cast-iron architecture in the States, just behind New York City's historic Soho District, you can find a concentration of characterful bars and clubs right in the heart of Portland's entertainment district, also known as Old Town Chinatown. One of which is, CC Slaughters, a neon lit bar, shirtless live dancers and strong music keep the night exciting, and the laser lit dance floor is always accommodating. The gay bar and nightclub features many themed and adventurous nights. Among them "Filthy Friday Party" certainly never disappoints.

🕐 1500–0200 daily
🏠 219 NW Davis St., OR 97209,
📞 +1 (503) 248 9135
f Slaughters Portland
URL www.ccslaughterspdx.com

"CC's is happening so it brings many different types of people to one spot – it's Portland so don't be rude and don't hate or you'll probably get kicked out."
– Martha Grant

52 Lovecraft Bar
Map F, P.105

Lovecraft is an eccentric bar located on the Eastside of the city. This horror themed bar is home to some of the best dance nights in the city according to locals. Its reputation could come from the surprises you may find inside throughout the night. With laser lights piercing through an almost entirely smoke machine filled dance floor to the rickety bar serving drinks expected from a dive bar, the decor feels like props collected right out of an 1980s slasher film. Lovecraft also hosts live music burlesque shows and tarot card readings.

🕐 2000 till late (Su-Th), 1600 till late (F-Sa)
🏠 421 SE Grand Ave., OR 97214
URL thelovecraftbar.com 🍷 21+

"Check out the Queer Monthlies if you're in town.
Turn up! And NecroNancy will get anyone dancing,
drinking, and probably laid."
– Donovan Edwards

53 Ground Kontrol
Map C, P.103

Ground Kontrol is Portland's top-notch classic arcade. Doubling its space and capacity in summer 2016, the arcade maze in historic Old Town draws crowds from all over the city to reminisce about the 1980s and 1990s' good old fun even those who never experience the period. Over 100 classic video games and pinball machines are maintained, with a full service bar serving beer, nibbles and themed libations. Have some change on you as there can be a long line for the change machine. Some nights the arcade also hosts DJ's, trivia nights, tournaments and Rock Band–based karaoke.

🕐 1200–0230 daily
🏠 511 NW Couch St., OR 97209
📞 +1 (503) 796 9364
URL groundkontrol.com
🖉 21+ with photo ID after 5pm

"Go for Donkey Kong, Mortal Kombat, Sunset Riders, cheap beer, with a pocket full of quarters."
– Mako Miyamoto aka Neon Werewolf

54 Goodfoot Pub & Lounge
Map G, P.106

Over two floors in Southeast Portland, Good-foot's offers craft beer, decent burgers, pinball machines and four pool tables to shoot around at its upstairs pub, and a prime list of Portland-based musicians and frequent residencies at its basement venue that opens mostly only for events at 9pm. Live funk and soul fill the lounge every Friday night so wear your dancing shoes and be prepared to groove the night away if you're up for it. Pool games are inexpensive but even so they're for free Sunday through Thursday.

🕐 1700–0230 daily
🏠 2845 SE Stark St., OR 97214
📞 +1 (503) 239 9292 URL thegoodfoot.com
🔗 Cash only, Make bookings 2 weeks ahead

"Cheap drinks, check. Sweaty basement, check. Prefunk beforehand, the party gets going late!"

– Kayla Hoppins

55 White Owl Social Club

Map F, P.105

Formerly a dive bar, White Owl Social Club is now a modern cozy, low-lit rocker bar with many of Oregon's local craft beer and spirits to included with its experience. The American bar cuisine accommodates many of the nutritional asks of its patrons, such as its signature kale slaw that adorns a few of their sandwiches. Adjacent to the interior is an equally spacious patio containing wooden picnic tables and a concrete fire pit for the evenings. During the lively months the bar hosts many events, DJ's, and parties that can be heard from blocks away.

🕐 1500–0230 daily
🏠 1305 SE 8th Ave., OR 97214
📞 +1 (503) 236 9672
🔗 www.whiteowlsocialclub.com
🎟 21+

"Our friends at White Owl have been throwing some of the best parties that the city has seen. And, the food is delicious. Lot of talent in those White Owl walls."

– The Pressure

 **56 Wake The Town
@The Liquor Store**
Map I, P.107

Often starring noted DJs or preluding major events, such as What The Festival, Wake the Town occurs monthly at the Liquor Store, with a first-rate lineup brought by two of the city's well respected underground selectors and Portland natives Barisone and PRSN. The night features hours of bass music with undertones of hip hop and reggae sounds unique to the duo's symbiotic sonic stylings. The Liquor Store itself is a hipster bar with a selection of well put together cocktails that are sure to keep everyone occupied.

🕐 *2200–0200 (Monthly last Thursday)*
💲 *Price varies with events*
🏠 *3341 SE Belmont St., OR 97214*
📞 *+1 (503) 754 7782* ⓕ *Wake The Town PDX* 🔗 *21+*

"This is such a fun party for me because it focuses primarily on GOOD dancehall music. It's a limited capacity, so make sure to show up before 11pm."

– Reva Maureen DeVito

57 Likewise

Map I, P.107

You might think that an all white walled space with art hanging all over the insides is a sign of a crisp hip art gallery. Instead it's an experimental bar that aims to support artistic pursuits in the bar scene. A bartender residency program, arguably the first of its kind, draws adept bartenders to concoct their very own cocktails and specials every two months, where patrons can enjoy at a long communal table perfectly placed for people watching. Find an item on the menu that presents an "experience" available once before it changes to a new one for purchase.

🕐 1600–2300 (Tu-Sa)
🏠 3564 SE Hawthorne Blvd., OR 97214
📞 +1 (503) 206 4884 🔲 likewise.website

"Where else can you go and order a drink from Garfield the cat, or people watch while reading a signed copy of Miranda July's latest book?"

– Jason Sturgill

58 Le Happy
Map D, P.104

A Northwest crêperie with a cozy Portland interior, Le Happy resembles a dining room full of a nostalgia with the smooth addition of a disco ball on the ceiling. Another twist is that Le Happy stays open later than the bars most nights providing classic French sweet treats, a few delectable salads, several craft beers and a full cocktail ready bar to end the night on. Best suited for dinners or late night meal, the French-styled haunt offers undeniably energetic vibes and a very unique appeal that draws quite a fun crowd.

🕐 1700–0000 (M-Sa), 1000-1430 (Sa-Su)
🏠 1011 NW 16th Ave., OR 97209
📞 +1 (503) 226 1258
URL www.lehappy.com

"It's by far the best crepe place I could recommend in Portland, not to mention a great restaurant in general. Try building your own crepe – I've never regretted it."
– Ryan J. Bush

59 Bula Kava House

Map H, P.106

Bula Kava House is Portland's first Kava bar providing fresh ground kava root from south of the Pacific where the tea-like beverage originates. Historically the drink is meant to treat pain and relieves forms of anxiety. It also provides a relaxing feeling, like an alternative to alcohol and other intoxicants for recreational purposes. Bula Kava House stays open till midnight and also provides a super healthy menu of juices, smoothies, and acai bowls alongside their fresh Kava selection.

🕐 1100-2300 (Su-Th), -0000 (F-Sa)
🏠 3115 SE Division St., OR 97202
📞 +1 (503) 477 7823
URL *www.bulakavahouse.com*

"Good vibes, quality Kava. Take some Kava chocolate to go."

– Kyle Banuelos, Stublisher Inc.

60 Stargazing
@ Mount Tabor Park
Map L, P.107

Mount Tabor is an extinct volcanic cinder cone that exists in a small neighborhood in the city. The peak of the landmark has 360-degree views of the city and all the surrounding mountains views one could ask for, and is also one of the best places in the city to look up at the stars. Its location makes the park highly accessible, even bike-rideable. There is a surprisingly lively nightlife with bars, pubs and cocktail lounges such as the Sapphire Hotel all to accompany the beautiful summer sunsets from the west hills.

◷ Pedestrians/bicycles: 0500-0000 daily, automobiles: 0500-2200 (Th-Tu)
🏠 SE Salmon St., OR 97215
URL www.taborfriends.org

"During the summer my favorite nightlife activity is to caravan up the hill with a bunch of friends, lay on our backs, and gaze at the midnight sky."

– Holly Andres

MAP A

Aprisa Mexican Cuisine

SE 9TH AVE
SE 10TH AVE
SE 11TH AVE
SE 12TH AVE

HOSFORD – ABERNETHY

SE DIVISION ST

21

APEX ●

SE 8TH AVE
SE MILWAUKIE AVE

Clinton St / SE 12th Ave

SE WOODWARD ST   1000 ft.

MAP B

SW KINGSTON AVE
SW ROSE PARK RD
SW SHERWOOD BLVD

Washington Park Amphitheater

5

International Rose Test Garden

1000 ft.

MAP C

NW JOHNSON ST   Jamison Square

NW HOYT ST

Up

Hap Gallery ●

NW EVERET

NW 13TH AVE
NW 12TH AVE
NW 11TH AVE
NW 10TH AVE

27   MadeHere PDX

Powell's City of Books ●

W BURNSIDE ST   Maak Le Courier Co

● Tanner Goods Retail Store

SW 13TH AVE
SW 12TH AVE

● Heart Coffee

Multnomah Whiskey Library
SW 11TH AVE   Frances

2   Galleria / SW 10th

2

Central Library   Director Park

SW SALMON ST

SW MAIN ST

1000 ft.

● 2_4T Trail
● 5_Portland Japanese Garden
● 21_Independent Publishing Resource Center
● 27_The Good Mod

- 9_Ira Keller Fountain
- 36_Portland Farmers Market @PSU
- 48_Caffe Mingo
- 58_Le Happy

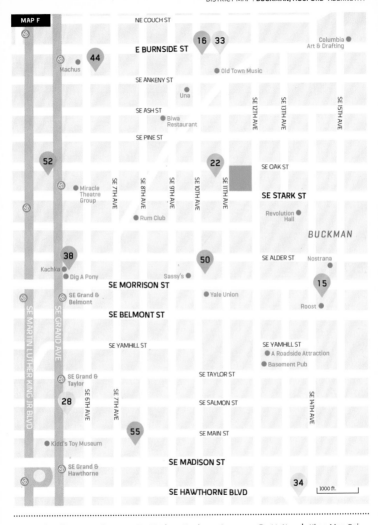

MAP F

NE COUCH ST
E BURNSIDE ST
SE ANKENY ST
SE ASH ST
SE PINE ST
SE OAK ST
SE STARK ST
BUCKMAN
SE ALDER ST
SE MORRISON ST
SE BELMONT ST
SE YAMHILL ST
SE YAMHILL ST
SE TAYLOR ST
SE SALMON ST
SE MAIN ST
SE MADISON ST
SE HAWTHORNE BLVD

SE 7TH AVE
SE 8TH AVE
SE 9TH AVE
SE 10TH AVE
SE 11TH AVE
SE 12TH AVE
SE 13TH AVE
SE 15TH AVE
SE 14TH AVE
SE 6TH AVE
SE 7TH AVE

SE MARTIN LUTHER KING JR BLVD
SE GRAND AVE

Columbia Art & Drafting
Machus
Old Town Music
Una
Biwa Restaurant
Miracle Theatre Group
Rum Club
Revolution Hall
Nostrana
Kachka
Dig A Pony
Sassy's
Yale Union
Roost
A Roadside Attraction
Basement Pub
Kidd's Toy Museum
SE Grand & Belmont
SE Grand & Taylor
SE Grand & Hawthorne

1000 ft.

- 15_Milk Milk Lemonade
- 16_One Grand Gallery
- 22_ADX
- 28_Wildfang
- 33_Hippo Hardware & Trading Co
- 34_Really Good Stuff
- 38_Oso Market + Bar
- 44_Nong's Khao Man Gai
- 50_Holocene
- 52_Lovecraft Bar
- 55_White Owl Social Club

DISTRICT MAPS : KERNS, RICHMOND, HOSFORD-ABERNETHY

MAP G

NE COUCH ST

35

E BURNSIDE ST

Screen Door

Luce

41

40

Laurelhurst
Theater

42

Smut Vintage

Cheese & Crack
Snack Shop

SE 20TH AVE
SE 22ND AVE
SE 24TH AVE
SE 26TH AVE
SE 28TH AVE
SE 30TH AVE

SE PINE ST

Ken's
Artisan Pizza

SE 29TH AVE

SE OAK ST

Penny Market

54

SE STARK ST

1000 ft.

MAP H

SE SHERMAN ST

SE CARUTHERS ST

59

45   SE DIVISION ST

Salt & Straw

18

Roman
Candle
Baking Co.

SE 25TH AVE
SE 26TH AVE

30   SE CLINTON ST

SE 28TH PL
SE 29TH AVE
SE 31ST AVE
SE 32ND AVE
SE 33RD AVE
SE 33RD PL
SE 34TH AVE

SE WOODWARD ST

1000 ft.

MAP I

56

● Khun Pic's Bahn Thai
SE BELMONT ST
● The Sweet Hereafter
● Aalto Lounge & Bistro
SE YAMHILL ST

SUNNYSIDE

SE 34TH AVE
SE 35TH AVE
SE 36TH AVE
SE 37TH AVE

SE MAIN ST

SE MADISON ST

● House of Vintage
57
SE HAWTHORNE BLVD
1000 ft.

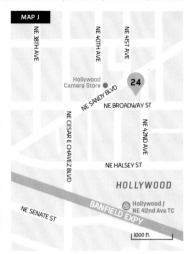

MAP J

NE 38TH AVE
NE 40TH AVE
NE 41ST AVE

Hollywood
Camera Store
24
NE SANDY BLVD
NE BROADWAY ST

NE CESAR E CHAVEZ BLVD
NE 42ND AVE

NE HALSEY ST

HOLLYWOOD

NE SENATE ST
BANFIELD EXPY
◎ Hollywood /
NE 42nd Ave TC

1000 ft.

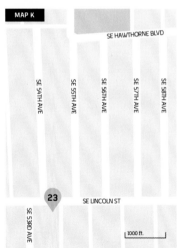

MAP K

SE HAWTHORNE BLVD

SE 54TH AVE
SE 55TH AVE
SE 56TH AVE
SE 57TH AVE
SE 58TH AVE

23
SE LINCOLN ST

SE 53RD AVE

1000 ft.

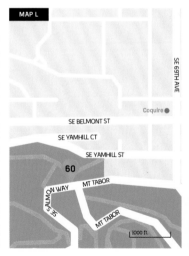

MAP L

SE 69TH AVE

Coquire ●

SE BELMONT ST

SE YAMHILL CT

SE YAMHILL ST

60

SE SALMON WAY
MT TABOR

MT TABOR

1000 ft.

- 23_The Lincoln Street
  Kayak & Canoe Museum
- 24_Hollywood Theatre

- 56_Wake The Town
  @The Liquor Store
- 57_Likewise

- 60_Stargazing
  @Mount Tabor Park

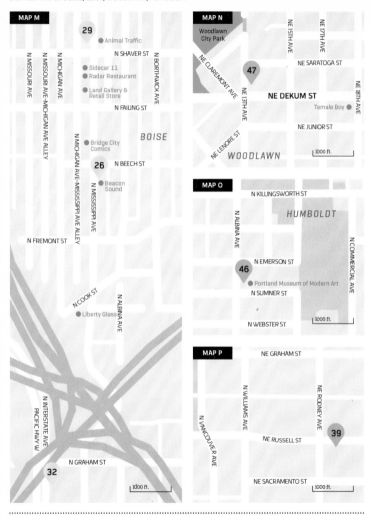

MAP M

29

● Animal Traffic

N SHAVER ST

N MISSOURI AVE
N MISSOURI AVE-MICHIGAN AVE ALLEY
N MICHIGAN AVE
N MICHIGAN AVE
N BORTHWICK AVE

● Sidecar 11
● Radar Restaurant
● Land Gallery & Retail Store

N FAILING ST

BOISE

● Bridge City Comics

N MICHIGAN AVE-MISSISSIPPI AVE ALLEY
N MISSISSIPPI AVE

26 N BEECH ST

● Beacon Sound

N FREMONT ST

N COOK ST
N ALBINA AVE

● Liberty Glass

N INTERSTATE AVE
PACIFIC HWY W

N GRAHAM ST

32

1000 ft.

MAP N

Woodlawn City Park

NE 15TH AVE
NE 17TH AVE

NE SARATOGA ST

47

NE CLAREMONT AVE
NE 13TH AVE

NE DEKUM ST

NE 18TH AVE

Tamale Boy ●

NE JUNIOR ST

NE LENORE ST

WOODLAWN

1000 ft.

MAP O

N KILLINGSWORTH ST

HUMBOLDT

N ALBINA AVE

N COMMERCIAL AVE

N EMERSON ST

46

● Portland Museum of Modern Art
N SUMNER ST

N WEBSTER ST

1000 ft.

MAP P

NE GRAHAM ST

N WILLIAMS AVE
N VANCOUVER AVE
NE RODNEY AVE

NE RUSSELL ST

39

NE SACRAMENTO ST

1000 ft.

● 26_Reading Frenzy

● 29_Worn Path

● 32_Beam & Anchor

● 39_Toro Bravo

● 46_Sweedeedee

● 47_P's & Q's Market

MAP Q

N BALTIMORE AVE

8

N PHILADELPHIA AVE

N CRAWFORD ST

Willamette River

ST JOHNS BRIDGE

N PITTSBURG AVE

1000 ft.

MAP R

N ARGYLE ST

KENTON

N WILLIS BLVD

17

Disjecta ●

N INTERSTATE AVE

N MCCLELLAN ST

N FENWICK AVE

N KILPATRICK ST

N SCHOFIELD ST

1000 ft.

MAP S

NW ST JOHNS BRIDGE

Willamette River

NW ST HELENS RD

3

NW BRIDGE AVE

1000 ft.

MAP T

SE 160TH PL

SE VILLAGE LOOP

43

SE MCGILLIVRAY BLVD

1000 ft.

MAP U

NE PRESCOTT ST

NE 87TH AVE

NE 85TH AVE

NE 86TH AVE

NE SANDY BLVD

NE 88TH AVE

NE WARD ST

7

NE SKIDMORE ST

1000 ft.

MAP V

HILKEY LN

14

BATES RD

Indian creek

1000 ft.

● 3_Forest Park
● 7_The Grotto
● 8_Cathedral Park
● 14_WildCraft Studio School
● 17_Carl & Sloan
● 43_Phở Lê

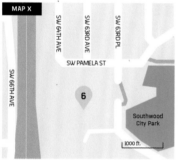

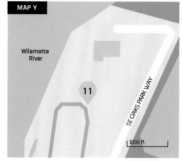

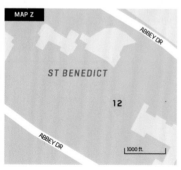

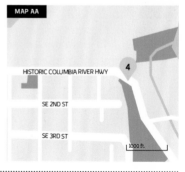

- 4_Columbia River Scenic Highway
- 6_Portland Oregon Temple
- 10_Willamette Falls & Municipal Elevator
- 11_Oaks Park
- 12_Mount Angel Abbey Library

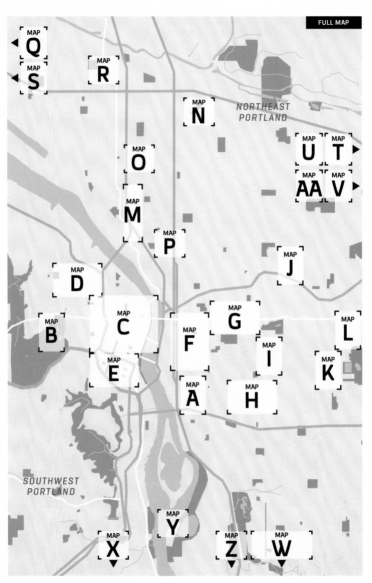

Accommodation

Hip hostels, fully-equipped apartments & swanky hotels

No journey is perfect without a good night's sleep to recharge. Whether you're backpacking or on a business trip, our picks combine top quality and convenience, whatever your budget.

 < $100 $100–250    $251+

Hotel Monaco

Lodged in a circa-1912 building, this centrally-located, designer-furnished hotel is a 12-minute walk from Portland Art Museum and two blocks from a MAX station that serves three light rail lines. All 221 retro-styled guest rooms come with Atelier Bloem amenities, Italian Frette linens, and hotel bicycles to borrow. WiFi is available for a fee.

🏠 506 SW Washington St, OR 97204
📞 +1 (503) 222 0001
URL monaco-portland.com

Ace Hotel Portland

In the heart of an emerging downtown neighborhood stands the 79-room hotel characterized by ample proportions, luminous spaces and a reassuring sense of early 20th century brawn. Feel Portland here at ease where local supplies, art and the smell of freshly ground Stumptown Coffee mingle at one place.

🏠 1022 SW Stark St., OR 97205 📞 +1 (503) 228 2277 URL acehotel.com/portland 💲

The Society Hotel

🏠 203 NW 3rd Ave., OR 97209
📞 +1 (503) 445 0444
URL www.thesocietyhotel.com

Jupiter Hotel

🏠 800 E Burnside St., OR 97214
📞 +1 (503) 230 9200
URL jupiterhotel.com

Travelers' House

🏠 710 N Alberta St., OR 97217
📞 +1 (503) 954 2304
URL www.travelershouse.org

Caravan the Tiny House Hotel

🏠 5009 NE 11th Ave., OR 97211
📞 +1 (503) 288 5225
URL tinyhousehotel.com

Notes

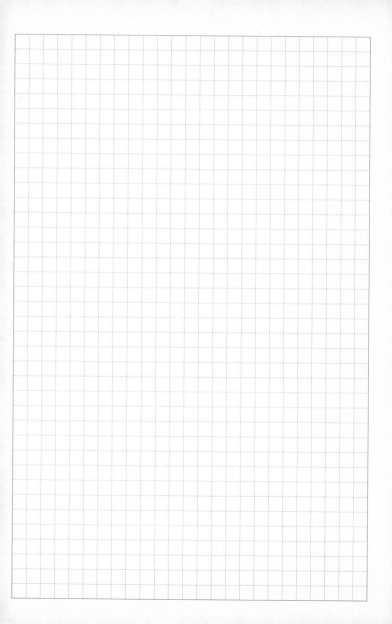

Index

Music

Photography

Photo & other credits

In Accommodation: all courtesy of respective hotels.

CITIX60

CITIx60: Portland

First published and distributed by
viction workshop ltd

viction:ary™

7C Seabright Plaza, 9-23 Shell Street,
North Point, Hong Kong

Url: www.victionary.com
Email: we@victionary.com
🔲 www.facebook.com/victionworkshop
🐦 www.twitter.com/victionary_
🐞 www.weibo.com/victionary

Edited and produced by viction:ary

Concept & art direction: Victor Cheung
Research & editorial: Queenie Ho, Caroline Kong
Project coordination: Jovan Lip, Katherine Wong
Design & map illustration: MW Wong, Frank Lo

Project management: Rey Robles
Contributing writers: Rey Robles, Kendall Henderson
Cover map illustration: Joyce Fan
Count to 10 illustrations: Guillaume Kashima aka Funny Fun
Photography: Kendall Henderson, Ikaika "Tiki" Cofer

Content is compiled based on facts available as of June 2016. Travellers are
advised to check for updates from respective locations before your visit.

First edition
978-988-13204-0-7
Printed and bound in China

Acknowledgements

A special thank you to all creatives, photographer(s), editor, producers, companies and organisations for your crucial contributions to our inspiration and
knowledge necessary for the creation of this book. And, to the many whose
names are not credited but have participated in the completion of the book,
we thank you for your input and continuous support all along.